Goldsworthy Lowes Dickinson

From King to King

The Tragedy of the Puritan Revolution

Goldsworthy Lowes Dickinson

From King to King
The Tragedy of the Puritan Revolution

ISBN/EAN: 9783743320239

Manufactured in Europe, USA, Canada, Australia, Japa

Cover: Foto ©ninafisch / pixelio.de

Manufactured and distributed by brebook publishing software (www.brebook.com)

Goldsworthy Lowes Dickinson

From King to King

FROM KING TO KING:
The Tragedy of the Puritan Revolution. By G. Lowes Dickinson, Fellow of King's College, Cambridge

> "Methinks I see in my mind a noble and puissant nation rousing herself like a strong man after sleep, and shaking her invincible locks. Methinks I see her as an eagle mewing her mighty youth, and kindling her undazzled eyes at the full midday beam, purging and unscaling her long-abused sight at the fountain itself of heavenly radiance"
>
> MILTON *in 1644*

PUBLISHED BY GEORGE ALLEN, 8 BELL YARD, TEMPLE BAR, LONDON; AND SUNNYSIDE, ORPINGTON. 1891

Amicus Amico

PREFACE.

THE pages that follow contain an attempt to state, in a concrete form, certain universal aspects of a particular period of history. The tragedy lies in the conflict of reforming energy with actual men and institutions; and it has been the object of the author to delineate vividly the characters of leading actors in the struggle, their ideals, and the distortion of these as reflected in the current of events. This is the general purpose of the work; to attempt to expand it, in detail, in a preface, would be to imply that the book itself is superfluous; for the dramatic form was deliberately chosen, because that of an essay appeared insufficient.

It is hoped that the unity of the whole series of dialogues is secured by the natural development of the subject-matter; this result, it is true, if it has been attained, will only be perceived by readers who have a general acquaintance with the history of the period; but such readers must be numerous, and it is to them, primarily, that the work is intended to appeal.

Accuracy in detail is not essential to the excellence of such a work; it has, however, been studied, though probably not with complete success. In forming his conception of the men and the period, the author has consulted the most recent authorities, whose names are too well and honourably known to students for it to be necessary for him to repeat them. It is his hope that he will not be found to have misrepresented the truth, by attempting to embody it in an artistic form.

KING'S COLLEGE, CAMBRIDGE,
March, 1891.

CONTENTS.

	PAGE
ELIOT AND HAMPDEN IN THE TOWER	1
LAUD AND CHILLINGWORTH	9
STRAFFORD AND HIS FORMER TUTOR GREENWOOD IN THE TOWER	19
LAUD IN THE TOWER	31
MILTON AND HIS FORMER TUTOR YOUNG	35
LORD FALKLAND AND EDWARD HYDE, AT THE HOUSE OF THE FORMER, GREAT TEW, NEAR OXFORD.	45
THE CAMP OF THE PARLIAMENTARY TROOPS AFTER NASEBY	57
THE KING AND HIS GROOM OF THE CHAMBER, THOMAS HERBERT, AT NEWPORT	73
CROMWELL	85
JOHN LILBURNE BEFORE THE COUNCIL	91
CROMWELL	101
CROMWELL AND VANE	109
VANE ON THE SCAFFOLD	119

I.

Eliot and Hampden in the Tower.

1632.

[*Eliot was imprisoned for his opposition to the Crown in the Parliament of* 1628. *His liberation was made conditional on an humble acknowledgment of his fault, which he steadily refused. He died in the Tower in the November of* 1632.]

I.

ELIOT. Yes, I grow pale! A breath of Cornish air
Would make this Tower a Heaven! Suppose the sea
Beat at its dripping base, and winds in tumult
With clang of birds and sailing foam-drift sang
Shrill by the cliffs and turrets; suppose Tintagel
Had been my prison, and yonder slit revealed
The huge Atlantic heaving, sun and cloud,
Moisture and ocean fragrance! Suppose, suppose . . . .

Enter HAMPDEN.

O sir, you are welcome!
  HAMPDEN.   Eliot! what a den!
Why have they changed your lodging?
  ELIOT.   My friends, they said,
Were wont to pay this poor conspirator
Too frequent visits for the kingdom's peace.
    HAMPDEN. You're looking ill. Have you physician
    here?
    ELIOT. One that prescribes me exercise and free-
    dom.

HAMPDEN. Does the king know?
ELIOT.   Doubtless.
HAMPDEN.   And makes no sign?
ELIOT. Why should he?   He waits for me as I for him,
And so will wait, till——   This is good-bye to you;
Henceforth they'll not admit you; take my thanks
Less for your gifts, though they were dearly welcome,
Than for the constant love which made them so.
HAMPDEN. I must not urge submission, else . . . .
ELIOT.   No, do not!
A man who cared to purchase life with honour,
Selling his country's freedom for his own,
Were not that Eliot, Hampden calls his friend,
Nor one whose liberty were worth the cost
Of turning keys to gain it. You know my judgment,
And where it errs will pardon; but an error
In spirit and purpose opens such division
As, though 'twere pardoned, is not reconciled.
If I should yield 'twere interest—not conviction:
You will not ask it.
HAMPDEN.   I should ask in vain,
If I could ask at all. And yet it shakes me
To see you thus. This chamber strikes like death.

ELIOT. Death's not the end, nor drawing breath on
 earth,
The sum of life; a moment, though in prison,
May tap the soul's eternity of freedom.
But tell me news! Does disaffection grow?
What of the church? what of a parliament?
 HAMPDEN. Of parliament no whisper even; the
 king,
Who never called one save to grant him money,
Finding his milch-cow restive locks her up
And turns to milk the bull. Tonnage and poundage,
Benevolences and loans—you know his methods.
 ELIOT. I've suffered by them, so may you! The
 church?
 HAMPDEN. Already's all but papist! There Laud's
 supreme,
As Wentworth in the state. Altar and surplice,
Crossing and genuflexion ape religion;
The war cry's "Uniformity," the weapons
Prison and fine. That little choleric man
Would stamp his fretful likeness on a nation!
 ELIOT. Do they submit?
 HAMPDEN. Do they? They've not forgotten
Queen Mary's fires at Smithfield! They'll lose their
 ears,
Their lives, if need be, but they'll not submit.

Beneath this cover of iron rule the state
Boils like a cauldron. Merchant, priest and lawyer,
Noble and squire meet, mutter, urge, debate,
An ocean round the throne, whose occupant,
Posing before his glass, complaisant fronts
The flatt'ring face of absolute authority.
    ELIOT. O and I'm here in prison! Hampden,
        Hampden,
Had I not passion, action, wisdom, words,
Had I not once? Did you not use me then?
Scarce forty-two! It's over young to die!
    HAMPDEN. Not yet! We need you!
    ELIOT.   Every one you need!
Is the king mad? Or does he think the glory
That gilds the head of God's imperial vicar
Will fire-transmute his fraud to justice? No
If earthly kingdoms stand by imitation
Of the immense and ordered universe,
Or if their wisdom be to copy large
The private state of philosophic spirits,
Then must their single head be one who moves,
Though absolute, by certain laws of reason,
As does the sovereign mind ; so were the king
A nation's providence, as God the world's!
But now—why, Hampden, this might breed rebellion!
Does no one warn the king? Has he no friend?

HAMPDEN. One here in prison.
　　ELIOT. 　　　　　A kinder one than Wentworth.
But my work's done!
　　　　　　　　Did you not laugh to hear me
Harangue as if you'd been the Speaker? Well,
A broken horse will prick his ears and caper
To hear the hounds! It's you that England looks to;
You'll not forget it, Hampden? I know you will not.
　　HAMPDEN. I've not the tongue, nor heart, nor brain,
　　　nor . . . . Eliot,
I'm half myself without you!
　　ELIOT. 　　　　　Hush, they're knocking,
Our time's concluded. Why, how cold you are!
You're not acclimatised to this new lodging
And now, farewell!
　　HAMPDEN. 　　God bless you, Eliot.
Send me your manuscripts.
　　ELIOT. 　　　　Then send me books!
Is it a bargain? Then, once more, farewell!

II.

Laud and Chillingworth.

June 30, 1637.

II.

LAUD. Well, is it over?

ATTENDANT. It is, my Lord.

LAUD. Let me hear, then! Was there a crowd assembled?

ATTENDANT. Immense, and immense the noise! When Burton's ears were cropped, the very houses shook. On all sides shouting and groaning, laughter, lamentations, oaths. There were men drunk and men sober, women of the streets and merchants' ladies, puritans, priests, 'prentices, bullies, beggars. Bastwick's wife was there; she took his ears and kissed them and laid them in cotton-wool; and the people cheered her home in triumph, till, as I hear, she fainted on the way. Burton carried a nosegay some woman had given him against the heat and dust. Presently, a bee alighting on it and beginning to suck the flowers, "See this poor insect," said he, "as she draws sweetness from my posy, so I in this place from my Lord Jesus Christ."

LAUD. They spoke to the people then?

ATTENDANT. Continually through those two hours. There were many who listened and answered; others were drinking, quarrelling and cracking nuts. "Come, sear me, sear me!" cried Prynne, "I shall bear in my body the marks of the Lord Jesus." They branded him twice on one cheek, but he made no sign of pain. He spoke much of bishops and of *jus divinum*—

LAUD. No matter for that! Did not the others flinch?

ATTENDANT. Not a whit; Bastwick no more than Prynne. "Had I as many lives," said he, "as I have hairs on my head, I would give them all for this cause!" And his carriage did but enforce his words.

LAUD. Ah! did you hear what comments passed in the crowd?

ATTENDANT. More than I care to repeat to your Grace.

LAUD. Well, no matter. You can go.

[*Exit* ATTENDANT.

"Wolf of Canterbury!" "Pope of Canterbury!" I know as well as if he had told me. That's a small matter, God forgive them! But that these men should be permitted to harangue the crowd! no precautions taken! a punishment converted to a triumph!

what hope of amendment where such oversights still obtain? None, I am sure, in my time! 'Twas but last night I dreamt I was a name pilloried in a circle of ink. Who knows what that may bode? No good, I am sure. God help us all! And now for three years the nightingale has been dumb in my garden at Lambeth. Her silence is more sorrowful than her plaint! Slander, weariness, age, and death! A melancholy sequence and close!

Enter CHILLINGWORTH.

LAUD. Ah, Mr. Chillingworth, I am glad to see you! you are from Tew?

CHILLINGWORTH. I am, my lord.

LAUD. You've strange company there, wits and divines, philosophers and poets. Beware of excessive disputation, 'tis the very curse of the time, when all will be talking and none doing. The Lord Falkland, they say, has a subtle mind?

CHILLINGWORTH. Too subtle, your Grace would hint?

LAUD. Not altogether so. Yet there are some would plane so smooth they plane away to nothing. Too fine a dissection may chance to sever the nerve it seeks to expose.

CHILLINGWORTH. Or shall we say, my lord, to

change the metaphor, truth is a sick man a breath of air may destroy? Best keep him in bed in the dark!

LAUD. Why, why, Mr. Chillingworth——

CHILLINGWORTH. Nay, your Grace is wont to allow me licence; else I might fare as hardly as Mr. Prynne and the rest whom I saw just now in the pillory.

LAUD. Ah, you saw them! And what were your thoughts?

CHILLINGWORTH. To be frank with your Grace, I debated with myself whether it were for punishment you had set them there; or whether you were not rather intending them, what they actually enjoyed, a higher pulpit and a larger congregation than any church could offer.

LAUD. This is scarcely a matter for jest, Mr. Chillingworth! The negligence you witnessed is criminal! There is no limit to the harm it may have wrought! It would be well if you could understand it so.

CHILLINGWORTH. I doubt not your Grace is in the right; but why set them in the pillory at all?

LAUD. Why, there it is now! You are an able and learned man, Mr. Chillingworth, but you live too much with your books. Let me tell you, what you ought to have known, that these are froward times and cry for discipline! Men run from government as if it were the plague! They make themselves as free in a church as a tinker and his bitch in an alehouse! They speak of an archbishop as they might of their mother-in-law! Decency is mocked as superstition; yet without decency is no religion and without religion no society. It is not for libelling me that these men are punished, but for libelling through me the church and the state.

CHILLINGWORTH. Well, my lord, I am no politician, but one thing I could never understand. That faith may create altars and surplices we know from experience, but on what warrant does your Grace hope to reverse the process? Though you bow a man's body at the name of Jesus you cannot enforce the adoration of his heart. Postures are no substitute for devotion, no more than kisses are for love. For it is not observance that generates reverence, but reverence observance; or, as our poet Spenser has it, "Soul is form and form doth body make."

LAUD. Good poetry, Mr. Chillingworth, but bad policy. Had you known the world as long as I, you would be aware that men are governed by custom rather than conviction. They act and think thus or thus, because thus or thus they have always acted and thought; resembling in their lives certain beads of glass I have seen at the court (Prince Rupert I think devised them); a single crack and they fly to powder; a single flaw in the sphere of habit, and religion, morals, civil obedience vanish in a moment into dust. To wise men, it is true, reason is the centre whereon their belief and action inevitably turn; but with them we have not to deal, they need no government. Our concern is with ignorance and vice; and these, being incapable of conviction, a customary ritual must direct.

CHILLINGWORTH. I understand! as the Jews were directed by the law which Christ abolished.

LAUD. Dear, dear, dear, Mr. Chillingworth, you take things too absolutely! Ceremonies are but a means of grace. He who is accustomed to bow his knees will the sooner learn to humble his heart (though you will not believe it). He who is familiar with the forms of prayer will the more readily comprehend its spirit. As there is one truth, so should there be one observance; our uniformity is but a means to unity, and unity . . . .

CHILLINGWORTH. Is the end of the whole creation! But unity vital, not mechanical! a creature self-moved, not a dummy pulled by strings!

LAUD. Well, well, well, that may be the end indeed,

but we are speaking of the means. How will you bring this unity about?

CHILLINGWORTH. In the book I shall have the honour to submit to your Grace I have endeavoured to define those fundamental points on which all Christians are agreed. Let these be the tenets of the church and the rest indifferent.

LAUD. Why, there you are again with your academic notions! For though your fundamentals be clear as day there will plenty be found to dispute them. You will take the Scripture as your basis, but where is the rule of interpretation? Reason, you will tell me! But whose reason? yours, or mine, or his? Reason itself is an art, like government, and how many are there who possess it? Trust me, Mr. Chillingworth, there will be as many divisions over your fundamentals as over all you hold indifferent. And more than that, there will be divisions over the Word itself. To invite men to judge is to invite them to doubt, and to doubt there is set no limit. Those who quarrel with the church will quarrel with the gospel, and blasphemy and atheism supervene upon dissent. If the Scriptures be the rule, the interpreter is the tradition of the church; the one form the piers of the bridge, the other the superstructure; and under flows the river of hell. You are silent, Mr. Chillingworth.

B

CHILLINGWORTH. My lord, what should I say? If we may not trust to reason, to what may we trust? Your Grace will answer, authority; but whither is authority leading us? Though I be a man of the study my window looks out upon the world, and I know (far better your Grace must know) how fast and hot indignation grows. Here a church window broken, there an altar destroyed; here a tumult in the services, there an abstention from them. Scurrilous tracts in all men's hands, libels affixed to the walls, and intruded in your very chamber. This is the unity authority enforces! How is it better than sects and schisms?

LAUD. Oh, Mr. Chillingworth, these are the troubles of government. We do but what we can, the issue is in other hands. Maintaining the authority of the church we maintain the bond of all society. If we fail (which God forbid!) the state fails with us. The monarchy stands or falls with the church, England with the monarchy. The cause is urgent indeed, and the sedition you describe (alas! too truly) calls rather for severity than relaxation. I would have you pray that strength and wisdom be granted to us all; for these are serious times!

III.

Strafford and his former Tutor Greenwood in the Tower.

May 11, 1641.

[*Strafford was executed the following day.*]

1

III.

STRAFFORD. Welcome, old friend and tutor! You
    are from Ireland?
How did you leave them?
    GREENWOOD. Well my lord, as might be.
Your lady bade me tell you, she remembers
Lord Strafford's wife must own Lord Strafford's
    courage.
"And yet," she said, "being my husband's lady
I owe him tears, which, whether owed or not,
I cannot choose but pay!" Yet still in public
Her eyes were dry, protesting incredulity
That he whose life was stamped, a priceless coin,
With the king's head, the king alive, should perish.
That was before . . . .
    STRAFFORD. Before the king's decision.
I know!—she is not ill then?
    GREENWOOD I left her well.
There are some tender flowers a dewdrop crushes;
She was not so; but even the stateliest lily
Hailstones will shatter.

STRAFFORD. Ah! And the children, doctor?
GREENWOOD. They sent their loving duty.
STRAFFORD.   I've written to Will;
He must learn patience with his sisters now!
Is he not turned-fifteen? O, I could wish
I were that iron they think me! There's a love
Passing the love of kings, else what a world!
There's little gratitude, Greenwood! Do you know
    me, doctor?
GREENWOOD. Know you, my lord?
STRAFFORD.   Why, I scarce know myself!
I never felt so! is it the constant pain,
Or mere inaction? Something's broken in me.
I could be passive now and talk philosophy,
As if all life were talking; I could doubt almost....
GREENWOOD. My lord, you are ill!
STRAFFORD.   No, no. What think you, doctor?
Shall I seem most a criminal or a victim?
GREENWOOD. My lord....
STRAFFORD. Not yet, don't answer! you shall hear
    me
Make my defence. Why, I must be myself
Before I die. Let me remember—so!
My life being made for action, like a stream
By ev'ry pebble chafed, too torrent-swift
To loiter wide in sky-reflecting levels,

Shot in its course direct. My birth and fortune
Impelled me first, zeal made that motion fatal.
I was ambitious; not as some who covet
Crowns their weak skulls are cracked by, but I knew
Each moment what I could, conforming still
To the tried strength and compass of my faculties.
I was so born to rule that He who made me
Would laugh to have seen me private; Paris of Troy
Was not with more impetuous wind of passion
Swept to his Helena than I to empire!
My nature such, remained the reason's office
To choose her means; and thus the matter stood—
The smooth harmonious motions of authority
(Whose offices are like the stars of heaven),
The calm and awful firmament of power,
Was shook with jars and jangles; and that sphere,
Which in its compass comprehends and governs
All the particular inferior orbs,
The king's sole power, disordered; whence what peril
To all below is patent. This being so
I, as mistrusting green opinions, sought
Advice from whom I could, till well confirmed
The cure was double; first to purge away
Those counsellors that fouled the royal source,
Next to cut off the still encroaching spurs

Of popular privilege, that so the stream,
Pursuing smooth an unimpeded course,
By many a grassy ditch and conduit brim
Might drench the parched acres. The first was done,
And I swam large in that exalted heaven
Where late the fav'rite blazed ; the rest remained
For me to do, and never bullet sped
With less divided aim ; for thus I reasoned :—
Society's a war, the king an umpire,
The laws his principles, whose settlement
The Parliament with him has power to order.
But should this Parliament, itself a party,
Carp at his judgment, flout his Ministers,
With impious hands snatch his compelling power,
Then the chain breaks, the pieces fly, the toil
Of centuries is lost, and ordered rule
Shattered in universal anarchic battle !
Reasoning so, and so being shaped by nature,
I took in hand this task, with what success
The king may judge, with what reward I know
To compensate for health and life undone.
Why, I was all one ache with public service ;
I neither slept nor ate ! You'll think I brag—
But that your Prynnes, and Pyms, and Bens, and
    Denzils,
Should call me traitor, me ! Let Pym's whole body

Try what my finger bore of daily business!
And yet—I half believed it at the trial.
The people's noise, the blaze of scarlet peers,
The pompous hall piled to the roof with faces,
Pym with his fatal jaw and finger point
Marking the tick of doom, and underneath
All flux of argument a single current
Setting with tideless motion to my death!
It shook my soul! That's over! Now I know
Myself and them! Whipped schoolboys, in rebellion
Against the birch! Why, I'm myself again!
They call me harsh; it's easy work to smile,
Though for such smiles a world shall come to
    weep!
I was to serve the king, not please his enemies!
I served him, and I die for him to-morrow!
There's my defence! Is it sufficient, doctor?
    GREENWOOD. To you, my lord, it is.
    STRAFFORD.   But to you, Doctor?
    GREENWOOD. My lord, it's over now. You lived
        and die
Strafford! I never wished it otherwise.
    STRAFFORD. Yes, but what think you of this
        Strafford?
    GREENWOOD.   My lord,
I think my thinking will not alter yours.

STRAFFORD. But still, your judgment? Let me
have your thoughts.
GREENWOOD. Why should you want them? Those
you wore in life
Are best for death.
STRAFFORD. No matter, let me hear you.
GREENWOOD. My lord, you shall. I think the Earl
of Strafford,
The greatest man alive, deserves to die.
STRAFFORD. And yet you love me?
GREENWOOD. Indeed I think I do.
STRAFFORD. What! love a traitor?
GREENWOOD. I did not call you so!
They banished Aristides for his justice,
And Strafford's loyalty may deserve the scaffold.
STRAFFORD. What! justly?
GREENWOOD. Justly!
STRAFFORD. This is philosophy!
GREENWOOD. My lord, you asked my thoughts!
STRAFFORD. Give me them further.
GREENWOOD. If I were apt to rail, and did not
know,
To curse the world were but to curse myself,
Your fate would make me bitter. Fashioned so
In every splendid power of heart and brain
To one sole end and purpose, so impelled

On with such vast and planetary motion,
Till in the perilous height of heaven's wide vault,
All in a moment quenched and dropped extinct
In a cold obscure sea, for no more fault
Than being that glorious creature you were made
By Him who now unmakes you—O 'tis common,
But pitiful, my lord, so pitiful!
    STRAFFORD. You said "deserves to die."
    GREENWOOD.   I pass to that.
You, this one man, set on a point of time,
The past and future judge, and all mankind.
You wrought as if immortal; promises,
Laws, precedents, were nothing; crash you went
Through every slow-built barrier raised to stem
The swift returning tide of despotism.
You knew the course, you meant to keep the channel
By your own free intelligent discernment
Of public good and evil—say you did,
What of your next successor? What should check
Him but the law? and law you swept aside,
Hurling the young creation back to chaos,
That you might recreate! You poured contempt
On the wise patiences of living time,
Crying "One man, one work!" And now you wait
Death with your work! The greatest man alive
Is hardly matched, my lord, against the world!

And yet there's more. You treated men as children,
Whom a kind father governs for their good ;
But children grow, my lord, to take possession
Of their bright heritage, reason, which to sway,
For good or ill, by force, betrays not love,
But most tyrannical folly. There's a spirit .
Sleeps in the grossest clods, which once awakened,
They'll soar as light as seraphs. You cannot kill it ;
My lord, it's killing you !

STRAFFORD. Indeed ! I fancied I was dying of spite
For being too good a servant ! But no matter !
For your indictment, if I understand it . . . .

 GREENWOOD. My lord, there's no indictment ! what
  you did
You had to do. These are not charges brought,
'Tis but yourself described. You bade me speak.

 STRAFFORD. 1 thought your words would shake me ;
  they do not.
Some later time may judge me ; for my own,
I served it as I could. Yet one thing troubles me,
Lest the king's service suffer.

 GREENWOOD.   The king's a scoundrel.

 STRAFFORD. You say so ? You a Pymmite ?

 GREENWOOD.   My lord, I'm nothing,
Only I know a scoundrel.

 STRAFFORD.   Call the king one ?

GREENWOOD. He signed your life away!
STRAFFORD.   Ten thousand lives
Aren't worth his finger! He's the vital soul
That kindles our whole body! To die for him,
Is dying for oneself! O, my old tutor,
My friends are his, his mine! No more, I pray you.
  GREENWOOD. My lord, your last sun rises; when he
    sets
I shall have lost the kindest friend I know,
And my one hero. Men to come will judge you,
This way or that; I neither praise nor blame.
Across my sober path one comet flashed;
I felt its warmth, was of its beauty enamoured,
Foretold and saw its ruin. O thus, thus,
The world can shape and shatter! Farewell, my
    lord.
Be the king what you will, and I your friend.

IV.

Laud in the Tower.

May 12, 1641.

IV.

LAUD. Is not the earl come forth yet?

ATTENDANT. Not yet, my lord.

LAUD. The noise of the people increases. It must be nearly time. Can you see nothing?

ATTENDANT. There are soldiers waiting at the door in the court; and, hark, the drums begin!

LAUD. Now, then, they must be coming.

ATTENDANT. There's a stir at the door, the soldiers form into ranks, the marshals and sheriffs emerge in procession. The warder follows, then a single gentleman, bareheaded, clothed in black; and next—yes, here is the earl.

LAUD. Quick then, let me come to the casement! Now, Lord, give him strength, and me!

ATTENDANT. They are marching slowly; will he pause? Yes, they halt at the window—he is looking up—God, what a face!

LAUD. [*From the window.*] Farewell, my lord! The grace of the Lord Jesus Christ, and the love of God, and the fellowship of the Holy Ghost be upon you and dwell with you always!

ATTENDANT. He bows and answers something. Now they are moving on. Ah! see the Archbishop! catch him! so, lay him down! a little water for the temples, and chafe his hands gently, so, so. Now his eyes open, he is recovering.

LAUD. I am well, I am well, let me rise! Gentlemen, you will think I fear death; but I trust, when it is my turn to die, you will see that I grieve more for the earl than for myself. And well I may! for neither I nor any churchman has served religion as he has. And yet, if I grieve, it is not for him alone, but for the kingdom fallen into ruin. God have mercy upon us all! Come, let us read the burial service; the earl must be already on the scaffold.

V.

Milton and his former Tutor Young.

In the Summer of 1641.

V.

MILTON. How beautiful it is! The stillness of this twilight hour is laden with voiceless orisons. The trees rise tapering, motionless and solemn, as aspiring in prayer to heaven. The limes exhale their richest fragrance, and evening primroses unfold their sweetness to the moon. She, poising her golden globe on the lower eastern slopes, looks full on the glow in the west that brightens still her mellower radiance. And though we miss the nightingales of June, the later night will find voice in the mysterious hootings of the owl. Each summer, I think, gains richness from those that went before, and the series of my quiet twilights at Cambridge and at Horton finds expression in this single moment of full and effortless existence.

YOUNG. My pupil, I see, is more a poet than ever.

MILTON. O sir, the title were an honour indeed! the poet is he who understands the world in its essence and origin, Love. The beauty he perceives and celebrates is the final expression of truth, and that which action and philosophy for ever seek, he in a moment arrests and fixes in enduring lineaments. His life passes out of himself into the larger life of the whole, whereby he is turned insensibly to virtue, following from the necessity of his nature the maxims the moralist enjoins. His aim and achievement is immortality, so that even while yet in the bonds of flesh, he is wrapt at whiles into the heaven of heavens, catching sound of those eternal harmonies, whose echoes alone inform his vital and inevitable numbers.

YOUNG. And when is the great work to appear? Is the plan of it yet conceived?

MILTON. I have imagined many themes, and of some sketched in the outline; but the late occurrences have shaped my hopes anew. The battles and triumphs of the past attract me no longer; rather my ambition would lead me (did my faculties but equal my desire) to celebrate the new-born sun of liberty, dawning already in cloudy pomp on this expectant island.

YOUNG. A worthy purpose! I would it were certain of fulfilment. But the vapours are gathering thick, and the noon may prove but a grey one. The old is not yet removed, much less the new established. The bishops still retain their titles and offices.

MILTON. But not for long! Nature and reason declare against them. Reformation is a living spirit that will have its way in the end. For years has this stubborn England resisted its creative stress; again and again resumed her accustomed deformity. But now the moment is come; the stuff, no longer rebellious, assumes of itself the new proportions, till suddenly it fronts the sun, a radiant and renovated creature.

YOUNG. A brilliant image! Let us trust events will conform to it. Yet I confess I have my fears. We shall win in the end, I believe; but who knows, in the struggle, what elements may arise to obstruct the Presbyterian settlement? Who knows . . . .

MILTON. But it is the spirit we must look to! Once but make men free, and their nature will make them virtuous. Remove but these trammels of compulsory ceremony, these vexatious episcopal courts, these monstrous endowments prolific of simony and sloth; give religion but leave to breathe from her swaddling-clothes of authority and use, and you shall no longer need to prescribe her form and limits. Herself will express herself as her vital essence directs, and the organised body accrete to the subtle motions of the spirit.

YOUNG. A fine conception! Yet we must take heed, after all, that this body conform to the Scripture type. There is (as must be known to a scholar like yourself) but one true and perfect model, accepted by all the reformed churches abroad, and especially by the Scottish nation. This it is all good men's purpose to establish; but there are many who would encourage anarchy for the sake of license, intruding their alien sects in the gap between two establishments. From the old to the new is a leap, not an orderly progression; and from that intervening gulf all dangers may be feared.

MILTON. But, sir, what dangers? What is it you Presbyterians dread?

YOUNG. We Presbyterians (among whom, I trust, may be counted my sometime pupil) have some of us acquired a larger and sadder experience than his. We have learnt how many that cry against bishops are such as would cry against all authority. They would resent the parochial censure no less than the episcopal fine, would act or speak, pray or abstain from prayer, at their own good pleasure, and give to every conventicle and meeting-house the allowance of a parish church. You have heard of the Brownists under the late queen? I had thought them long ago suppressed, but already in a single year their congregations have revived by scores; from Holland and from the West come fanatics more dangerous still; there begins to be talk of toleration, of . . . .

MILTON. And what better talk were possible? Toleration! it is but a name for charity!

YOUNG. Such charity as ends in hell! Why, sir, would you tolerate Popery?

MILTON. It is not a faith, but a policy.

YOUNG. Or atheism?

MILTON. That God himself condemns.

YOUNG. Why, then, my young friend, let us hear no more of toleration; for error is error still, be it great or small. There is but one truth, and to miss it by an inch is no better than to miss it by a mile. Condemn atheism, and you condemn implicitly all seemingly minor errors.

MILTON. That I would gladly dispute with you; but we should but mar the night with angry altercation. Let us therefore postpone our difference and pass to a less contentious argument.

YOUNG. As you will, as you will! though I scarcely think your cause will be bettered by the most prolonged meditation. However, it grows damp and chilly, and perhaps it will be more prudent to retire.

MILTON. If you will go before, I will join you
within an hour.

[*Exit* YOUNG.

MILTON. How still it is! No stir of gustier air
Shakes in the leaves, no nearer sound obscures
The distant noise of watch-dogs; odours stream
Unhindered through the windless atmosphere,
The stars burn steady, nor does aught of cloud
Darken with shadowy drift the pacing moon:
O'er heaven and earth expectant silence broods
With charmèd wings, and casts her spell on me.
Spirit of sacred light, whose silver throne,
Mid lesser stars obsequious, cloudless hangs ·
Staining the violet vault of night; O thou,
Who once, from Heaven descending, didst illume
With hallowed altar-fire and tongues of flame
Thy chosen saints of Pentecost; on me,
Though later born, to utt'rance less divine,
Such grace bestow as, kindling all within,
May prompt prophetic song, not all unfit
To celebrate thy people's praise and thine!
For now, too long despaired of, dawns at last
Our consummating day, which, ushered drear
With wind and scudding cloud, or, more disastrous,
Battered intolerably by rattling tempest,
Or amber-lit, serene, and crystalline,—

Howe'er it dawn, O may it break at last
To such excess of noon as,—Father of Heaven,
Dazzling, eternal, Lord of angel hosts,
That azure fire let no intruding shade
Quench into night! rather with heavenly flame
Sustain its mortal substance!   Purge and prove
Thy people's heart! give them a single purpose!
That so their acts, wedded to prayer and praise,
May blend harmonious concord, apt to charm
Even angelic ears in Paradise :
Where round the burning throne eternally,
Seraph to seraph, saint to saint responsive,
With silver trump and harping symphonies,
Peal in a choir immortal hallelujahs.
To such attune, though weak, my mortal voice,
That, while this island-nation, born anew,
A golden eagle, beats her dauntless wings,
Undazzled, full, against the blaze of noon,
I, with not too presumptuous aim, may sing
Her praises right, nor, honouring her, forget
To celebrate, as due, Thee, sole Supreme,
Thee first, Thee last, and Thee eternally!

VI.

Lord Falkland and Edward Hyde, at the house of the former, Great Tew, near Oxford.

January 1642.

VI.

FALKLAND. What, Ned!

HYDE. Lucius!

FALKLAND. Have you business with me that you've ridden so far through the snow?

HYDE. And pleasure! Why did you leave me without a word?

FALKLAND. I thought you would hinder my going, and that if you needed me you would easily conjecture my hiding-place.

HYDE. It seems I have! Are you alone here?

FALKLAND. Except for ghosts! It was them I came to look for. This is the room, Ned, there is little change in it. That's Hales' chair in the corner; how the firelight used to dance in his dubious eyes! There sat Chillingworth; he was like the nightingale; when he sang the rest of us kept silence; even Suckling, the eternal talker, held his peace, who else was never still, but turned and turned like a wheel under stress of a torrent of words: doggrel, prose, blank verse, anything you would, except sense. And here's

Ben's throne in the centre, an Atlas to that heaven of flesh and wit. Was ever so bright a spark buried in bulk so mountainous? Yet that spark he would blow and blow till his whole body was fire. His very belly spoke like a god; it rumbled thunder to the flashes of his eloquence. They're merry ghosts, Ned, but I've no heart to jest with them. We'll have in the lights and fall to business.

HYDE. The dusk's a sad time in the winter; I could well feel regret myself. Yet those, after all, were but play days and bound to come to an end. There's more satisfaction in serious affairs.

FALKLAND. Less in the action than in the preparation. For me, I've met no pleasure in life but knowledge, wit, and love. Action is but gambling and gambling's tedious. One plays better than another, but all are at the mercy of the cards. If men were points in space, and passions mechanical forces, there would be some profit in experience. As it is, your wisest man is no better than a fool. An inch or a mile out, it makes no difference.

HYDE. Why, this is the old Lucius of Tew, whom I thought dead and buried! What has become of the impeacher of Finch? the shaker of Strafford? the outter to shame of bishops?

FALKLAND. Left in town, with my wardrobe. My

soul lives here, Ned, and I am come to see if it still remembers me.

HYDE. Would it might forget you for ever, if this be its temper! For it is the Falkland the Parliament knows that the king has need of now.

FALKLAND. The king!

HYDE. The king calls you to office. Why do you laugh?

FALKLAND. Because the king will make a Minister of his bitterest foe!

HYDE. Nay, Lucius, this is serious business.

FALKLAND. Oh, I am serious. For though I be not his bitterest foe I shall seem so to him. I shall oppose his heart's wishes, give him no flattery, laugh when he would be pathetic, be grave when he would jest, shrug my shoulders at his pleadings of conscience, rail at his bishops, approve his Commons, resist his accesses of tyranny, show him unmercifully the man that's hidden under the royal robes. And all this for what? For the pleasure of adding another piece to a game none understands but the invisible master that plays it! I wasn't made for a politician, Ned.

HYDE. What you were made for your talents and position best declare. There is no more eloquent speaker in the House, none of more instant and conquering energy. You have an estate and title, and the bravest heart in England, and but for these quibbling subtleties may rank among the soundest intellects. You cannot lie hid; meteor or marsh-fire, you may take your choice. Let me remind you briefly how things stand. The reformation we schemed and prayed for, before the Parliament's summoning, is more than accomplished. Lord Strafford and the rest removed, the archbishop in prison, the Star Chamber and High Commission abolished, ship-money made illegal, and the revenue in the Commons' hands. Correction now is finished and the balance hangs even again. But there are some would go further and give the preponderance to the other side; they would abolish the bishops, they would have Parliament control the Executive. Now is the very turn of the scales, and we, whose desire from the first was equilibrium, by siding with the king do but maintain our party while we seem to change it. We are and have been both for king and Parliament. As we opposed Strafford once, so do we now oppose Pym; we're for the mean against either extreme. This was your own expression; you chose to act in that interest and you cannot draw back now. If the king's power fall, and you inactive, it is you who have caused it to fall. You do not love the king—no matter! It is the office, not the person, we support. This I have spoken as a politician, let me speak now as a friend. I have a heavy burden to bear, and one that is likely to grow heavier. The king's a hard master for one who would do him good, and there are those in the House, moreover, who begin to call me traitor. In all this you have been my constant comfort, and the perfection of our friendship is matter of common fame. If you will join the same service your comfort to me will be so much the greater. But I would not urge you for that cause alone, did I not think your own good name and the kingdom would benefit. Consider it well, I beseech you.

FALKLAND. Am I to answer at once?

HYDE. As soon as may be. I would I had found you anywhere but here. You have let your thoughts escape to the blank outside of the world; recall them, I pray you, to the business of this planet, for they are like to make as little profit as they meet hindrance in the empty regions of space.

FALKLAND. I might take years to consider, and yet my choice be as foolish as though it were a moment's birth. Leave me for half an hour and you shall have my answer. You have no doubts yourself, Ned?

HYDE. None.

FALKLAND. Most happy Ned! In half an hour then.

Now, who would be a thinker? Yet who can
 choose?
There's no most common weed, no speck of dust,
But looked at closer leads the advent'ring mind
Sheer to abysms of doubt; and shall a kingdom,
The slow deposit of tidal generations,
A time's defeat, a centuries' epitome,
A still-unfolding bud, by dewy sweat
And frequent bloodshed watered—shall this miracle
Be sport for guessing children? Why, so it was
 made,
The makers knowing not how, and so it will grow!
Grow to what? There's the question! how to judge
'Twixt Parliament and king? These tedious words!
There's some would make this solemn house of spirits,
This calm caerulean music-haunted world,
A shop of government, all sweet repose
Broken by buzzing engines! Oh, I would let
A dummy rule, so I had bread and leisure!
Yet there it lies; 'tis seeking bread and leisure
Men fall on strife and hunger, giving birth,
Even in the act of flight, to what they fled from,
Still from the dawn of time engend'ring fire,
As natrium does, from water. Madness all!
Which some, as I, behold before they share,
Cassandra-like, in vain. For lo, what comes!

This blessèd isle, with all its congregation
Of friendships made and making, this Elysium,
Whose willow-glassing streams and flowered fields
Invite to love and contemplation, this,
Which like a spirit sings in the cuckoo's voice,
Breaks into war, whose issue, win who may,
Is but defeat! Oh, I could laugh—no matter,
I'll join it! What should I else? Am I not one
Among these tipsy livers? Do I not use them,
Eat the same bread, breathe the same breath as
   they?
Are not my goods their gift? My very leisure
The present of their toil? Have I not limbs,
Heat, motion, passions, even as others? Oh,
While I have flesh let that immortal prisoner,
The too-disdainful reason, folding up
Her azure-cleaving pinions, learn to draw
With other hacks this human caravan!
I join them then—which side? Where all are losers,
What matter? Despotism or anarchy,
The mean's lost either way! Yet for the king
Stands my best friend, one who perchance has eyes
Where I am blind; astronomers, they say,
Fall into ditches, so may speculators.
Ned shall persuade me—yet, for such a king!
Make me his Minister! Well, then, I'll be one!

I'll give him all my thoughts; I'll drive them home;
He shall have counsel and no flattery;
There shall be one man honest! One whose purpose
By too much thought was vexed but not perverted;
One who will die unhappy, yet with hope
That somewhere, when these creaking wheels are still,
In more majestic realms of ampler light,
Reason and love being met shall bring to birth
The life our own in mere distortion figures.

HYDE. [*Enters.*] Well, are you resolved?

FALKLAND. Do I not look it, Ned?

HYDE. You accept?

FALKLAND. Nay, what if I refuse?

HYDE. Why—you refuse, and the king and myself are sufferers. You are not resolved, then?

FALKLAND. Indeed I scarcely know. How serious you are, Ned!

HYDE. Nay, Lucius, time presses. Let me have your answer.

FALKLAND. In a moment; but why this haste? Consider, Ned; never again can we recall this instant of suspense. While I say "now" it is possible to imagine that two alternative courses are open. A moment hence, and there will stretch before us the long monotonous road of a single purpose; and that we must pursue to the end, without even the consoling certainty that it is leading to the goal we desire. What toys we are, Ned! Why should we not enjoy the jest as well as he who devised it?

HYDE. Oh, Lucius, where is the jest? The issue is simple enough; there can be no real doubt.

FALKLAND. Well, Ned, I'd rather travel with you than alone, however dreary the road.

HYDE. You accept?

FALKLAND. I accept. But why this jubilation? I have but accepted death. You do not fancy the king's is the winning side?

HYDE. Lucius, this place has infected you. It' sas sad as Acheron. Your woods are stocked with owls and ravens. For God's sake, let's be going!

FALKLAND. I am ready. The horses, quick! You need not fear me, Ned, for I leave my soul behind me. And so, for London!

VII.

The Camp of the Parliamentary Troops after Naseby.

1645.

VII.

I.

A SOLDIER. But why this anxiety for a regular ordained ministry? "Eldred and Medred," we are told, "prophesied in the camp." And Moses said: "Would that all the Lord's people were prophets."

PRESBYTERIAN MINISTER. A prophet is not the same as a preacher, see 1 Cor. xii. 28. But that I will not press. Prove me that your army preachers are prophets, and I won't quarrel about their ordination. But fluent discourse is not to be mistaken for the inspiration of the Spirit.

SOLDIER. Still less is mechanical learning, and a knowledge of Scripture. What else should testify of the Spirit but His presence felt within?

PRESBYTERIAN MINISTER. "Believe not every spirit," says St. John, "but try the spirits whether they are of God."

SOLDIER. Well, all that I urge is merely the liberty to try them; whereas you would predetermine the question by an external test of ordination.

PRESBYTERIAN MINISTER. And I have good authority. See Acts i. 21, 22: "Wherefore of these men must one be ordained to be a witness with us of his resurrection."

SOLDIER. What does that prove? That was a special case; besides, who knows what "ordained" may mean? There is nothing said of a formal ceremony.

PRESBYTERIAN MINISTER. There, too, I have you! Acts xiii. 3: "And when they had fasted and prayed, and laid their hands on them, they went their way." Here we have the description of a formal act. See also Acts xiv. 23, and many other passages to which I might refer you.

SOLDIER. Doubtless you can quote *ad infinitum;* so could I if I had as good a memory. And what comes of it all? I have heard divines dispute; they will cap citations by the hour or the day; and what is gained in the end? Each interprets the Scripture in his own way, and proves with sufficient ease the theory he is predetermined to believe.

PRESBYTERIAN MINISTER. Do you deny the authority of the Scriptures?

SOLDIER. I don't say that I do; but I believe my interpretation to be as good as yours. I mean no offence. I respect you as a good man, if not as a minister; but I maintain I have learnt more from the preachers you despise than from all the company of your brethren.

PRESBYTERIAN MINISTER. You are a foolish and presumptuous young man, and deserve the censure of the church. You confess your ignorance of the Scripture (for what else is your defective memory?) and yet you set up to judge its expositors. What says St. James? "My brethren, be not many masters, lest . . . ."

SOLDIER. There you are again with your pat quotations. If you had fought and felt as we have, you could never talk thus by the book. Religion is a thing not of words but of the heart. And it is to men like you, who never felt the passion of liberty, that we, who have staked our lives, are to submit! How can you understand us? Go your own way, if you will, but leave us free to go ours.

PRESBYTERIAN MINISTER. My young friend, there is but one way, and only the Scriptures can reveal it. Let me instruct you further.

SOLDIER. You cannot instruct, at best you can but silence me. But that you shall not do either. If such as you be the only Christian ministers, then am I and my friends no Christians. Keep you your steeple-houses and endowments; we will set up our congregation in the fields, and our liturgy shall be the prompting of our hearts. We do not seek to compel you; do you not seek to compel us, or you will suffer in the end.

II.

FIRST OFFICER. You speak as though our labours were over. On the contrary, they are only just beginning.

SECOND OFFICER. How so?

FIRST OFFICER. We have now to make terms with the king. It was easy enough to defeat him; but he'll be a very Proteus to secure.

SECOND OFFICER. Why, what can he do? He is bound to accede to our demands.

FIRST OFFICER. A king is bound to nothing; that's the beauty of his position. Besides, the more completely he is subdued the more numerous are the friends that will spring to raise him; pity is the surest provocation of loyalty, as envy is of rebellion. Vanity is concerned in both cases; in the latter directly, in the former indirectly; for the next best thing to being a king is to help to make or restore one. Similarly the next best thing to performing good works is to exhort others to perform them; a truth which has been largely discussed and practised in the camp of late, and which ....

SECOND OFFICER. That isn't the subject of our present discussion.

FIRST OFFICER. True, but it is a much more interesting one. However, I submit to your suggestion. You spoke, I think, of "our demands;" I'm curious to know who "we" are. You, for instance, in your heart of hearts, incline to a republic.

SECOND OFFICER. But I am willing to waive all that. What I contend for practically is the due predominance of the Parliament.

FIRST OFFICER. Precisely, and on no one of those three words "due," "predominance," "Parliament," will you find half a dozen men in the camp to agree with you. Oh, yes, yes, I know, don't interrupt! Of course all rational men must agree with you; I never met a man with whom it was otherwise; and that is precisely what has forced me to the conclusion that there is no such thing as a rational man. That being so, there is no reason for supposing that any one in particular will agree with you. So much for the political question; as to religion—why there, there's not even an attempt at concealment; I have only to run through a list of names, Presbyterians, Independents, Anabaptists, Seekers,

Familists, Ranters! all these are to have a share in formulating "our demands," while meantime, it may be worth remarking, that it is the Scotch, not we, who are at present in possession of the king, and are likely to claim a voice in the conditions of his reinstatement.

SECOND OFFICER. What a dismal croaker you are!

FIRST OFFICER. Not in the least; I'm perfectly cheerful; the situation interests me.

SECOND OFFICER. Have you no faith, no convictions?

FIRST OFFICER. That, as you remarked just now, is not the subject of our present discussion. But I'll answer your question by another. Did you know the Lord Falkland?

SECOND OFFICER. Him that was killed at Newbury? By reputation only.

FIRST OFFICER. I knew him; he was a wise man.

SECOND OFFICER. On the wrong side.

FIRST OFFICER. If so, he had at least the grace to be unhappy there. They tell me that as the war proceeded he lost his wonted cheerfulness, neglected his dress, grew careless of food or drink, spoke not at all, or only with a sharp intemperance; and, starting at whiles from melancholy reverie, would frequently ingeminate the burden "Peace! Peace!"

In battle, as he was careless of danger, so he cared not to kill, but rather to succour the wounded, till at last, as one who was weary of life, he deliberately laid it aside in the thickest of the fire at Newbury.

SECOND OFFICER. I wish he had belonged to us.

FIRST OFFICER. It was his nature to belong to nobody.

SECOND OFFICER. What made you speak of him now?

FIRST OFFICER. You asked me if I had no convictions.

SECOND OFFICER. Enigmas, as usual! I have never yet been able to learn your opinions on any subject.

FIRST OFFICER. Then you have failed to make an exceedingly unimportant discovery. I, on the contrary, have been formally introduced to yours, and do not particularly value the acquaintance.

SECOND OFFICER. You are frank!

FIRST OFFICER. That, however, does not prevent me from valuing yourself. As a proof of which I'll give you and your friends a piece of advice. Make terms with the king as soon as you can, if he'll let you. For the only alternative is to cut off his head, and submit to a new tyrant. And who that will be I think I may venture to prophesy.

SECOND OFFICER. Who, then?

FIRST OFFICER. Nay, that's my secret, which it would be premature to disclose. And now come down to the river and bathe. I assure you there's more satisfaction in a swim on a summer's day than in all the battles and policies of the world. Come, my dear boy. Be sensible for once.

III.

FIRST SOLDIER. Who's that fellow in black?

SECOND SOLDIER. The minister from Coventry, Baxter.

FIRST SOLDIER. What! the priestbyter?

SECOND SOLDIER. The blessed divine sent to undeceive us. Oh, what reformation we shall see! What salvation for Church and State! Hi, Mr. Bogster, or Bugster, or whatever your name is . . . .

FIRST SOLDIER. Don't bring him here, you fool! If he's like the rest of them I have had enough of their damned early-church parish-popery rigmarole.

THIRD SOLDIER. Oh, come, don't swear now.

FOURTH SOLDIER. Swearing's strictly forbidden. Hurrah!

THIRD SOLDIER. Poor chap, I'm afraid he's drunk.

FOURTH SOLDIER. All drunk in the Spirit! Shake hands, old man! All drunk together!

THIRD SOLDIER. In the Spirit, he says. I wonder now . . . .

FIRST SOLDIER. Oh, put him under the table. It'll be bad for him if the General comes this way. But as for this Baxter, I've been thinking we've had enough of these Presbyterian gentlemen. For my part I'd as soon be under a bishop as an elder; it's only a question of changing masters. And as to the primitive model taken straight out of the Bible, why, who cares . . . .

SECOND SOLDIER. That's what I say—who cares? There's some men now who talk of the Bible as if there were only one book in the world. Well, I say, I'd engage to write as good a one myself to-morrow. New men, new light, that's what I say.

THIRD SOLDIER. Yes, there's a great deal in that. These later days—that's what we must think of. It was only the other day I heard a fellow preaching about it. "In these later days," says he, that was his expression, these later days—"the Spirit's within us," says he, "not without."

FOURTH SOLDIER. Hear, hear! Spirit within us!

THIRD SOLDIER. "Well, then," says he, "the

Scripture's a dead letter." There's a great deal in that. There's some now who talk of reason . . . .

FIRST SOLDIER. Pity there aren't a few more!

THIRD SOLDIER. Well, I don't know now. It always seemed to me there was something worldly about reason. Not that I quarrel with any man . . . .

FIRST SOLDIER. Well, no one quarrels with you, and that's as it should be; you think as you like and I think as I like. But then comes your Presbyterian and says: "You think as I like!" that's what I complain of. Let him set up his church and let me set up my church, and neither of us pay for the other's religion. That's what I call fair.

THIRD SOLDIER. Well now, that does seem fair.

FIRST SOLDIER. No tithes, no endowments, no corporations!

FOURTH SOLDIER. No—nothing! Hurrah!

SECOND SOLDIER. Hear, hear!

FIRST SOLDIER. Stop that fool's mouth! What's the good of saying: "Hear, hear!"? You don't understand what I'm after any the better. What do you think you've been fighting for, all this time?

SECOND SOLDIER. Pay, I suppose.

THIRD SOLDIER. Oh, come now . . . .

FIRST SOLDIER. So have you, so have half the army!

But now I'll tell what I and my friends have been fighting for.

SECOND SOLDIER. What's that?

FIRST SOLDIER. A political settlement. Let the creeds settle themselves as they can. There's only two things we have to make for—a republic and toleration.

THIRD SOLDIER. Really! Well now, what do you understand by a republic?

SECOND SOLDIER. One man, one vote, to begin with.

FOURTH SOLDIER. One man, one vote; one vote, one pot; where's my pot?

FIRST SOLDIER. But that isn't all. If we get our way there'll be a fair division of property made, to say nothing of the land. What have they done with all the bishop's revenues? Are they to go to the new priestbyters? This war has been fought by poor men, and poor men ought to gain by it. That's what I want you men to understand.

THIRD SOLDIER. But we must remember, you know, that man doesn't live by bread alone.

FIRST SOLDIER. He doesn't live without it, anyhow.

THIRD SOLDIER. Well, there's a good deal in that, too. It's not that I want to dispute! What I feel is, that all you fellows are so sensible, I scarcely know whom to believe. It's wonderful in these later days (and that's what we must think of) what peace and good-will . . . .

FOURTH SOLDIER. Good-will! who'll swill? No drink, can't think! No . . . .

SECOND SOLDIER. Shut up! Well, I'm all for a republic and toleration. Let every one do what he likes, that's what I say. There's some men are all for morality, but what's morality? When all's said and done, what *is* right and what *is* wrong? There was a fellow preaching here the other day—one of these Ranters—and, says he: "If a man's in a state of grace," says he, "he can do no sin; the moral law," says he, "isn't what believers want." In a state of grace! that's where it is.

FOURTH SOLDIER. Shake hands, old man! All in grace together.

SECOND SOLDIER. You! why you're drunk! [*To* FIRST SOLDIER.] What are you laughing at?

FIRST SOLDIER. Why, if he's in grace he's not drunk; or if he's drunk, it's no sin!

THIRD SOLDIER. Well, now, that seems reasonable.

SECOND SOLDIER. Well, who said it was sin? He can be as drunk as he likes for all I care, it's his own business!

THIRD SOLDIER. Still, you know, there's all this talk about hell-fire; we can never be sure . . . .

SECOND SOLDIER. Oh, as to that, who can tell? I heard a fellow talking yesterday, who doesn't believe there's a soul at all. "For," says he, "what is the soul? If it isn't the body, what is it? Did you ever see it?" says he; "well, then, let's have no more talk of hell-fire!" And that's what I call reason.

THIRD SOLDIER. Well, there's a good deal in that. I never thought of it before from that point of view. It's wonderful, in these later days, what a number of opinions . . . .

FIRST SOLDIER. As many opinions as there are fools. I don't know if you're a friend of the Ranters, but I can tell you of a respectable woman who joined them and was carted through the streets the other day as a common whore!

SECOND SOLDIER. What's that to do with me?

FIRST SOLDIER. More than you'd care to own, perhaps.

SECOND SOLDIER. [*Strikes him.*] Take that then, for a . . . .

THIRD SOLDIER. Oh, come now—Hush! Here's the General!

[*Enter* CROMWELL.

FOURTH SOLDIER. Red Noll, scratch his poll! Shake hands, old man!

CROMWELL. That man's drunk—he's discharged!

What's the matter here? You are of Colonel Rich's troop, I think? He shall hear of this!

[*Exeunt* SECOND and THIRD SOLDIERS.

[*To* FIRST SOLDIER.] Stop, sir! I know your face. I met you in the battle. What have you to do with men of this kind? You fight well; it's a pity you cannot talk less.

FIRST SOLDIER. It's little enough we're likely to get either for our fighting or our talking.

CROMWELL. Why, sir, what would you have? Is it your pay?

FIRST SOLDIER. That, and a proper settlement of the nation.

CROMWELL. The settlement rests with the Parliament.

FIRST SOLDIER. I say it rests with us! and I'm not the only one to say so!

CROMWELL. You talk too much, sir. You can go.

VIII.

The King and his Groom of the Chamber, Thomas Herbert, at Newport.

November 1648.

VIII.

HERBERT. Sire, Colonel Cooke has returned from the castle.

KING. Well?

HERBERT. He found there were strangers in possession, and could get no further information. The rain and the heavy roads may excuse his delay in returning.

KING. It is indeed a rough night! Cannot these guards at the door be somewhat further removed? This gusty wind blows the smoke of their matches into the very chamber.

HERBERT. I have done what I could, but Major Rolfe was in bed, and it's hard to make him move. This is an anxious night. How does your Majesty?

KING. Oh, I have known worse chances than this. Set another light in the bowl, Herbert, for we shall hardly sleep to-night. What do you think this new arrival means?

HERBERT. I cannot tell; perhaps they intend to

transfer your Majesty elsewhere. I understand they are under orders of the army, not of the Parliament.

KING. The army! A second abduction by some Joyce? Just now that would be vexatious. The treaty with the Parliament went so smoothly I had hoped to reach a settlement; or, at least, to appear to do do so, till some opportunity of escape shall offer. And now, if the army interfere, they ruin all. This place is convenient, too, for taking ship, should I be driven to flight. I should be sorry to be transferred. Yet, who knows what the army may offer? Some more advantageous terms, perhaps.

HERBERT. They could not well be worse than those your Majesty has been driven to accept. To yield the control of the militia for twenty years . . . .

KING. That, I must tell you, was but a trick, to gain some necessary time. Why, if I had really intended that concession I should retain but the name of a king.

HERBERT. Yet I fear that neither party will be satisfied with anything less. And there is the question of episcopacy . . . .

KING. That I will never abandon, unless it were in appearance; and even so, perhaps, it were a sin. For, besides the obligation of my oath, I am fully persuaded that the government by bishops is that which is commanded in the Scriptures, and was practised by the early church. That is a point of conscience, therefore, which, under no compulsion, will I yield.

HERBERT. Of that I am well assured; and for that very reason I fear a settlement will never be concluded.

KING. Ah, friend Herbert, I see you are no politician, and so, for your better consolation, I will explain the grounds of my hope; for, if I am more cheerful than you on this dreary night, it is because I have a longer vision, and expect with good reason to escape from this dilemma without detriment to my authority or conscience. We have, as you know, two parties to deal with, the Parliament, which is Presbyterian, and the Army which is Independent; in the matter of religion, therefore, I am certain, if I displease the one, to gratify the other; if I refuse to establish Presbyterianism, I have the support of the army, and if I refuse to encourage the sects, I have the support of the Parliament. One party, it is true, is for abolishing episcopacy; but the other is content to preserve it on condition of a general toleration. Both would have me resign the militia for a time; but it is possible, under the stress of their mutual jealousies, that the period may be indefinitely reduced. Thus, while I stand in the centre and balance these opposing interests, every dispute is a gain to me, and it may well result that in the end, when they are wearied with perpetual intrigue, I may determine myself the conditions of my freedom.

HERBERT. Your Majesty understands these matters as I can never pretend to. Yet, suppose that one of these parties acquire undisputed predominance? For my own part, I confess that I fear the power of the army. How completely it has routed the Scotch, on whom, but six months ago, reposed our main reliance.

KING. That was unfortunate! and the more so, as they divided the Presbyterian interest, and introduced into our enemies' counsels an element of national jealousy. I was dashed, I admit, by the battle of Preston. Cromwell is a fine soldier!

HERBERT. Oh, sire, a terrible man.

KING. Why, not so terrible, after all, but that a man may manage him. At Hampton Court, I led him as I chose: tact and a clear head will do more than you imagine, Herbert. I wish he could have been one among the Parliament's commissioners here.

HERBERT. Yet they say he and the army are all against the treaty.

KING. Against this treaty, perhaps, but not against

one of their own negotiating; and that, I suspect, is the meaning of to-night's occurrence. The army will carry me off, and treat with me on their own basis. Indeed, what else can they do? A king is an awkward prisoner. He can neither be released, nor exchanged, nor put to death!

HERBERT. God forbid!

KING. Why, Herbert, what a doleful face! One would think you were already witnessing my execution.

HERBERT. Oh, sire, on this matter I cannot jest.

KING. Why, what other treatment is it fit for? You would not have me serious about it?

HERBERT. I beseech your Majesty's forgiveness; the long watches, and this night of wind and rain have disturbed my judgment. Something, too, I heard . . . .

KING. Well, well, what did you hear?

HERBERT. I am not sure; perhaps I was mistaken —I . . . .

KING. Speak out, man! I'm not a child.

HERBERT. It was from the guards in the antechamber—they were speaking of some remonstrance from the army to the Parliament.

KING. Well, what of it?

HERBERT. It contained some demand . . . . I thought I heard them say so . . . .

KING. I am waiting.

HERBERT. They had presumed, it seems, to demand —yet I cannot believe it—to demand that your Majesty be brought to trial.

KING. Be brought to trial! Why, Herbert, they must be mad, or you must! Be brought to trial! I! a king! Why, who should try me, and for what? Come, come, Mr. Herbert, you exceed your license.

HERBERT. Oh, sire, your pardon, it was but . . . .

KING. Not that you are to suppose that this is new to me, that I have never considered it. How that cursed rain beats! Will it never be dawn again? What was I saying? Yes, yes—I have considered, I say, I have tried to imagine whether it were possible for subjects to presume to judge their king; but no, I could not conceive it! For how? By law? The king is above the law! By force? A murder then, no execution! And, following that, what miseries upon the kingdom! What horror of princes throughout the world! What dissensions at home! What disastrous wars abroad! Religion with government in a moment overthrown; uprooted justice, security, morals: a blot where was a kingdom! No! no! not all the folly, all the crime, all the godlessness, even of these rebel factions . . . . Herbert, do you hear me? Don't stand and stare like a dolt!

HERBERT. Alas! your majesty . . . .

KING. You think I fear for myself, perhaps? Did you ever know me a coward? No man should die more royally! But my kingdom, the precious heritage I should have transmitted in undiminished glory! What will become of it? To whom will it pass? Why, Herbert, I could pity myself! Was ever a king so bent upon his country's good—so wholly set to maintain religion and authority? What has been my fault? That I have striven to uphold as I received it, I will not say mine, but the king's prerogative. For the king is more than I, or any man. He stands for God upon earth, by the continuity of long succession, imitating eternity in time. His will, though free and self-contained, moves in a natural accord with every righteous law. It is his to protect, his to initiate, his to dispose; on him, as ultimate base, repose the orders and relations of all society. Shatter him, and the State's enormous fabric, compact and welded by centuries of labour, crashes through in a moment to the empty night of chaos. That king am I, those powers I hold in trust; I will not yield them, Herbert! You will say I have done so; but it was in seeming only, and for safety; I told the queen so, would she but believe me! When I am free—if I am free—I must be free! Where were England without me? Herbert, can't you speak? Man, man, why do you weep?

HERBERT. To see your Majesty so discomposed. Indeed, I think there is no cause; doubtless all will go well, and the only ground for my fears was the love I bear your person.

KING. Well, well, well, happen what may, at least my conscience is clear. A blessed thought! except, except—now, Herbert, I will make you my confessor; and forgive me my roughness, for I believe you love me. One thing there is that troubles me—the Earl of Strafford . . . .

HERBERT. Oh, sire, it was an honour to die for your Majesty.

KING. I think he thought so, and yet—he had my promise. There is the misery of a king. He must put his country before his servants and his friends. As a man I would gladly have saved the earl, but as king I was forced to condemn him. My policy, my very throne, called for the sacrifice. Do you remember the mob about Whitehall, hour after hour, implacable, clamouring for his death? I cannot forget it—would I could! He was a good servant; somewhat imperious, perhaps—displeasing to the Court, and indeed, in part, to myself. Importunate, too, he was, as if he laboured for reward. Still, a good servant, and I would he were alive ; he might have saved me now—that is, if there were danger. A king's is a sad life, Herbert ; but his help, as all men's, is above. See, the day dawns at last ! I will go to prayer awhile, and then, if it may be, to sleep.

IX.

Cromwell.

December 5, 1648.

[December 6 was the day on which Colonel Pride "purged" the Parliament of the members who were still for treating with the king, in order to secure a majority in favour of his trial. Cromwell arrived in London on the evening of the 6th. The king was executed in the following January.]

IX.

CROMWELL. Is this a king? Then from such kings
    deliver us!
Who, on this sea of troubles, like a gull,
Skims the mere froth, or, diving, dives to prey,
While others ply perforce the royal task,
Mining the fundaments whereon the state,
Rock-reared, may soar an island. This a king!
Whose subtle brain, whose gravity and patience
Cloak but a gambler's heart! Yet time was given;
We reasoned, urged, besought, betrayed almost
The cause we stood for, lest, for one man's sin,
We be constrained to pluck that star from heaven
Our fathers durst not lift their eyes to. Oh,
If the bright diadem on England's brow,
Whose triple jewel held the world's eyes at gaze,
In the third place where blazed the royal stone
Must show an empty socket; if this tower
From Time's slow spoils with strain so huge upreared
As promised an immortal consummation,
Must in a moment crash, then be the blame

His where it's due, the king's, and we exempt!
For twice the Lord has spoken, twice our hearts
Answered amazed; to treat was human folly
Stemming the tide with brooms; which heeding not us
Bore us to Preston field resistless, and on,
Foaming to flood, on to the king's death! No,
We could not—if we would—oppose an ocean!
Authority's from God :—the ord'nance, true,
But the particular disposition man's,
Who, as he makes, unmakes; so, though the world,
Holding its breath a moment's shudder, then,
With universal shout of execration
From kings and dazzled peoples fling to heaven
A thund'rous charge to damn us—why, even then,
A few poor men will dare appear and answer it!

Yet were it time for fear there's cause enough;
My heart's friend Robin questions, Vane has doubts,
The Parliament's against it; whom if we force,
Levellers and anarchy! if we submit,
No guarantee for conscience! Then, say some,
Patience, have patience! Oh, I could well be patient!
I love my peace as others, fever and wounds
Rack me no less, calumny seems not sweeter,
Nor resolution easier; if peace were all,
I could lie down to die and count it happiness!

But, while we wear our flesh, there's contradiction,
Action and counter-action; 'tis the law
Makes life itself another name for battle,
And labels peace death. If we retire
'Tis not to rest but suffer, take the blows
We've merely ceased to ward; if that were all
We might make shift to bear it; but that the soul's
Immortal chalice, where the wine of God
Flashes Him back His heaven's perennial splendour,
That this should risk pollution, this be shook
From glassing as it may the face of Christ,
And whirled in muddy tumult! Oh, no, no,
Not while I live! What! the free act of prayer
Timed like an hour-glass, rules prescribed to conscience,
The torrent of faith bound in a formal bed,
And for the least divergence prison and fine
Portioned by wrangling priests! Not while I live!
Patience be theirs who own it, I'm for action!
Yet—Robin doubts, so many doubt, good men too!
To force a Parliament—to kill a king—
Then—what? Were reason all, I too could pause,
Doubting myself; but reason, being but human,
Is variable as men are. Never an act
But had some argument to recommend it,

And some, as good, against; the last decision
Speaks in the soul, where God speaks. Sudden events
Call for as sudden choice, whence faith is born
To mock at calculation. Who set me here
General of all the troops from Huntingdon?
Who planned, proposed, succeeded? Who? Not I,
Nor any man! 'twas God who, using me,
Wraps his own ends in darkness. I resist?
I were a fool! Though all men stand and question,
This way and that, one shall make bold to act.
To-morrow Pride shall do it, no stop for me!
Perish the king! If ever a man deserved
Death, it is he! And what shall happen next,
Why, let it happen! We do but what we can,
And where we err, may dare to ask forgiveness.
To London, then! The tide is near the flood.

X.

John Lilburne before the Council.

February 1649.

[*Lilburne was one of the leaders of the democratic faction known as Levellers, and the author of "England's New Claims Discovered," a pamphlet directed against the Government of 1649. For this he was summoned before the Council of State, and sent to prison to wait his trial.*]

X.

THE USHER. Your hat, sir.

LILBURNE. Hat! what hat? What men are these?

USHER. The Council, sir.

LILBURNE. The Council! who are they?
I see some members of the House of Commons;
This is to them. [*Removes his hat.*

BRADSHAW. Lieutenant-Colonel Lilburne,
The Council sends for you to make enquiry . . . .

LILBURNE. Sir, by your leave, it's I must put the questions!
What warrants forty casual gentlemen,
Privately met, to send a public force
And hale me through the streets against my will?

BRADSHAW. Sir, you mistake, you stand before the Council.

LILBURNE. What Council?

BRADSHAW. Those the Parliament appointed.

LILBURNE. And by what right appointed? This is a claim

New to our law, which makes the executive
A power distinct. And for this Parliament,
Since 'twas the king that called it, with the king
Ends its authority. Those officers
The people need, let them appoint themselves!
 CROMWELL. Sir, you are not to call our power in
   question.
 LILBURNE. Oh, am I not? I humbly crave your
   pardon!
Your majesty should charge it less to malice
Than ignorance, if men, whose blood and treasure
Were spent for liberty, forget at times
They've won no more than you may please permit
   them.
 CROMWELL. [*To* BRADSHAW.] Can this be borne?
 BRADSHAW. [*To* CROMWELL.] Patience! we'll sound
   him further.
Sir, you mistake the General, who, so far
From grudging liberty, desires to hear
(So do we all) the claim she makes through you.
What are these ends you and your party seek?
 LILBURNE. Not what we find without the pain of
   seeking,
New chains to bind us! Sir, you'll find me blunt;
My nature's so; John Lilburne never feared
To speak his mind to beggar or to king!

JOHN LILBURNE BEFORE THE COUNCIL. 95

You ask about my party; sir, I've none!
I lead the people, who, by nature free,
In course of ages, subjugate to force
Or gulled by fraud, have let their birthright go
For less than pottage! Thus do rich and poor,
Rulers and ruled, divide the groaning earth,
Till suff'ring breeds resistance. So we fared
In England, so rose up and killed our tyrant,
Whose empty place ('tis history's constant course)
Our leaders self-imposed would fain usurp.
Why, sirs, how monstrous! What's this Parliament,
To rule us all with councils and committees?
A factious knot of landed gentlemen,
The remnant rags of privilege! What's their right?
Election? Those who chose them gave their votes
Under the king that's dead; and those elected,
The greater part, are since removed by force.
Property? Why, what's property? there's some
Label it robbery! Yes, you may knit your brow!
We'll vex you yet, Lieutenant-General Cromwell!

BRADSHAW. Be temperate, sir, or silent! you forget
Our place and yours! you speak by sufferance.

CROMWELL. [*To* BRADSHAW.] Suff'rance too long!
we've heard enough, dismiss him!

BRADSHAW. [*To* CROMWELL.] No, let him show his
hand, we're safer so.

[*To* LILBURNE.] You blame the House; what are
  your own proposals?
LILBURNE. That you should ask! Why, they're in
  ev'ry mouth!
They're liberty's, not mine! Make conscience free!
There's some would play the bishop still, that all
May buy with tithes their patent creed and service.
Why if I chose to hail the rising sun,
As Persians do, or bow to pewter pots,
What's that to them? God be the judge, not they!
We'll have no Presbyterian parish popes,
No, nor no King, nor lords, nor council either,
But such a Commonwealth as renders law
A mere superfluous form, and poverty
An idle hieroglyph whose sense is perished.
These propositions aren't my own and private;
There's thousands make them; every troop has men
That eat and drink and sleep upon them; one
Cries from the grave to urge them. General Cromwell,
Arnold, you thought, was dead; I tell you, no!
He lives in every regiment! yes, and will,
Shoot whom you may! from every drop of blood
A hero springs to front you! Gentlemen,
Immortal justice is not slain with bullets!
  CROMWELL. [*To* BRADSHAW.] These are mere words!
  it's time we came to business.

BRADSHAW. [*To* LILBURNE.] Enough, sir, that will do. Now to the point.
Do you know this book?
   [*Hands him a copy of " England's New Claims Discovered."*]
LILBURNE.   I've heard some talk about it.
BRADSHAW. And know the author?
LILBURNE.   Know him?
CROMWELL.   Sir, to be brief,
Had you a hand in it? We know you had!
   LILBURNE. Is this an inquisition? By heaven and hell
I'll not reply! You'd best bring in your torture!
Star Chamber use demands it! Do your worst!
John Lilburne's not the man to fling away
His own and England's liberties for fear!
I know, because I'm Semper Idem John,
Who never yet for threats or flatt'ry changed
My constant principles; because I'm still
The poor man's shield and scourge of all oppression,
Therefore you'd have me silent! Never, never!
Truth speaks from prison and coffin! Late or soon,
What I say now the peopled world will echo!
   BRADSHAW. Enough, enough, sir!
      [*To the* USHER.] Let him wait without.

LILBURNE. Do what you will! But first a word of
  warning!
If, when all pretext fails, as fail it will,
You make recourse to martial law to judge me,
Then, by the great and living God I swear,
Appoint what prison you will, Whitehall, St. James',
I'll burn it out to ashes! These officers
Aren't fit for honest men to trust their lives to!
                                                    [*Exit.*
CROMWELL. Now are you satisfied?
BRADSHAW.   A dangerous man!
VANE. There's truth in what he says; this liberty
Is all we seek; the saints in heaven are equal,
So should the saints on earth be; would they were!
CROMWELL. Yes, but they're not, they're not! To
  hear him talk
All might be saints! Why, if it went by votes
Our heads would garnish Westminster to-morrow!
These men are worse than traitors; give them leave,
They'll ruin all! best silence them in time.
VANE. And so begins again the violent course
We rose to end. Once set that wheel in motion,
'Twill roll and roll till those who guide it, caught
Round with the whirling rim, are crushed them-
  selves
Under their own machine. Some of us here

Partly approve this fellow; where he errs,
'Tis zeal misleads him. Is he impolitic?
He does not frame our measures. Is he stubborn?
Let failure teach him wisdom. To shut him up
Argues the charges true that force must answer.

CROMWELL. Authority's a farce if men like this
Defy the Council. Break, or else be broken!
Such mean and blust'ring rogues to bring to ruin
The cause that's judged a king! I say, the Tower!
There let him wait his trial.

VANE.   I say, release him!

BRADSHAW. Your votes, then, gentlemen! Release
or no?
The General has it. Let him wait his trial.

XI.

Cromwell.

April 20, 1653.

[*The day of the violent dissolution of the "Rump" Parliament. A message was brought to Cromwell that its members were hastily forcing through a Bill whereby they would themselves retain their seats in the new Parliament, and also form a Committee of Revision to determine the validity of the fresh elections. It is this message that is supposed to interrupt the following soliloquy.*]

XI.

CROMWELL. Ambitious! that's the cry! That fellow
    Lilburne!
I hear him still, mouthing his beagle music
At us poor foxes! God be judge between us!
Who set me here? The testimony's palpable!
Naseby and Preston, Dunbar, Drogheda, Worcester,—
Why, the thing speaks! The army's me, the State
Me, the Lord's cause, me, me! And if the Lord's,
Why, let them break me who can, or shiver them-
    selves!
Ambitious! What have I done? Nothing! And
    shall do
Nothing! 'Tis all done through me! Take the
    worst,
Say I dissolve the Parliament, and fell
This the last pillar left of three that bore
The soaring roof, authority—say I do,
What follows? "Tyranny," they cry. Well,
    tyranny!
'Tis but a name; the thing's all! Tyranny!

Say I do not—why then "perpetuate"
Is all the cry; perpetuate this mere Rump,
These three-score shreds torn from the purple robe
New-woven in '40! These shall patch and tag
Our new State garment! Men who stood with me
On Dunbar field and chanted victory
Down the first level sun-shafts, honest fellows,
Who held their blood cheaper than some their oaths,
Must take their freedom at such men's discretion
As mete God's truth by inches, making conscience
A legal pint-pot good for all the land,
Nor more nor less capacious. Meantime the laws,
Through years of sloth run riot, wait their pruning;
The sheep cry out for shepherds; Church and State
Visibly ruin—and these men make their parties,
And cry "perpetuate"! How are they a Parliament
More than I king, or as much? A tyranny!

Ah, Harry Vane, I hear you! Continuity,
An equal suffrage, annual parliaments,
And all the saws of theory! good things, too,
Did not the sick times poison them to ulcers!
Were wind and waves an engine moved by clockwork,
And storms a mimic jest for yawning sailors,

Then might the pilot leave his slipp'ry post
And nod with grazing farmers, whose slow days,
Most like their slow streams, creep, in endless levels
Of labour generations long, to nothing.
If ifs were facts! Here's one, with small regret
Would doff the rude salt trade his forty years
Were somewhat stiff to dress in! Yes, friend Vane,
If ifs were facts! But lashed to the mast, and dinn'd
By all the horrible winds that e'er made crack
Heaven's vault to let the fire through—then to be told
Of constitutions! Oh, there's some would prate
Under the crack of doom!
For, Harry, think! Had there been one engagement,
But one, wherein we failed, this thing had been
Less palpable! but that these poor mechanics,
Ostlers and cast-off serving men, by nature,
And daily use, unwarlike, set to fight
With gentlemen should show like Roman heroes—
Were a man blind such testimony as that
Might give him eyes! 'Tis the plain spirit of God!
We must not grieve Him, Harry! Perpetuate! No,
'Twere plain denial of Providence! What then?
What were the worst that even Vane could fear,

The very worst? Come, let me speak it out!
Forced loans, imprisonment, knife and pillory,
Parliaments intermitted, the swift course
Of justice made a standing lake to drown
Acres of wealth, and breed—not cleanse—pollution;
England's whole state a suicide, whose hands
Pluck at her eyes, whose eyes mislead her feet,
While the blind feet go stumbling down to hell
As to a kitchen-warming—and to this madness
Cromwell not Charles the brain!
Yes, there I touch it, Cromwell now, not Charles!
Tyrant's as good a word as Parliament;
And, for the thing, good in each kind is better
Than bad in the other! Charles was false, but I?
Should I be? How I talk, when e'en this hour
The Parliament perhaps incline to reason!
If not—Oh, where is guidance? God in heaven!
"As is thy strength, so shall thy day be"—yes,
Amen, Amen!
   [*Enter a* MESSENGER *from the Parliament.*
    Well, sir, your message? Quick!
Well, what, what, what? Speak, blockhead! Now,
  do you say?
They're at it now? O monstrous! Harrison!
Half of them cheats, adulterers some, I know them!
I'll teach them! Harrison! Is Harrison there?

Quick, man, your hat and cloak! I'll do it now!
These sods, these money-bags, these wag-tongue
    legalists,
These moral lecherous censors, these saint-gaggers,
These bellies stuffed with bribes and stale plu-
    ralities,
These lips, these maws, these eyewhites! These are
    men
To rule the Lord's great England and his saints!
Gentlemen, who's for the House? Come, let's be
    going

XII.

Cromwell and Vane.

August 1658.

[*Cromwell's daughter, Lady Elizabeth Claypole, died on August 6, 1658. Vane was imprisoned in 1656, for his tract entitled "A Healing Question." Cromwell died on September 3, 1658.*]

XII.

CROMWELL. How still the house seems now she's
    dead! God, God!
Bore I so light a burden then already
That this, too great for man, was added? Oh,
Such pain! Could no one comfort? None allieve?
Must all sit by and watch it? Oh, no, no,
Too much, too much! Never to recognise me,
But speak of blood and vengeance! Alas! my child
Were there not foes enough to hate thy father
But thou must learn their language? Yet were it
    curses
Speak but once more, once! Never, never, never!

Where are these papers? Pamphlets, always pam-
    phlets!
"Arch-traitor" "Judas," "Cain"—how glib it runs!
"In godliness there is great gain, and preaching and
praying well managed will obtain other kingdoms as
well as those of heaven." "A deep dissembling hypo-
crite, as barren of all charity as hell is of honesty,"

and so forth and so forth. These abortions spawned in the dark! Here's another with his cry "Anabaptists, Seekers, Familists, Antinomians, Anti-Trinitarians"—the Presbyterian note!—" all these do grow and flourish under the shadow of his apostacy. While the one true church, the model ordained of Christ Himself, set up by His apostles, and without change maintained through the best and purest times, till Constantine . . . ." So, so, so, and now for his peroration! " Darkness is hid in his secret places ; a fire not blown shall consume him; it shall go ill with him that is left in his tabernacle. Though his excelling mount up to the heavens and his hand reacheth unto the clouds, yet he shall perish for ever like his own dung. They that have seen him shall say where is he!" Here's more and more of them! The Millenarian with his talk of anti-Christ and the immediate coming of the Lord—I would it were so! These are foolish men, less wicked than lunatic. The Leveller with his annual Parliaments, and every man his vote. And still it's " Oliver the usurper," " Oliver the oppressor of the poor," till there comes one with admonishment to kill me outright, since " in the black catalogue of high malefactors few can be found that have lived more to the affliction and disturbance of mankind."

What things are men! O God, I'm weary of it!
When my son died it smote me like a dagger,
And now my daughter! Thus laid bare of love,
Naked to face this howling storm of passion!
What man could bear it? Not a friend, not one!
[*Enter* VANE.
Yes one, one still! Harry, my brother Harry!
What man, you bear no grudge?
  VANE.   My Lord Protector,
Twas not my own affairs that brought me hither.
  CROMWELL. Why, let your business wait then.
    Tell me first,
They lodged you well at Carisbrooke? No roughness,
No incivility? It vexed my soul!
Why did you force me, Harry? It vexed my soul!
  VANE. My Lord Protector's soul is vexed too often
By acts himself imposes on himself.
  CROMWELL. Harry, you know it's false! The time
    constrains me.
  VANE. Was it the time expelled the Parliament,
Dissolved your own assemblies, though select,
Parcelled the land in Roman provinces
Under the soldiers' rule, distorted justice,
Sequestered, fined, imprisoned, made of Cromwell
An illegitimate Charles? Was it the time?

CROMWELL. You shall not vex me, Harry. I will not answer,
Or not at present; tell me of yourself.
    VANE. My lord, 'twas England's business brought me here.
    CROMWELL. My lord, my lord! Why then, Sir Henry Vane,
You came to speak to me of such a people
As from Algerian sands to these white shores
Has swept the sea of pirates; taught Savoy
That not unmarked in the Waldensien vales
The blood of saints crimsoned his Alpine snows;
And, far as Santa Cruz, to Spanish papists
Witnessed a power as proud as once of old,
For cause so good, to shatter as empty shells
Their huge and ocean-chafing armaments!
    VANE. "People," you said; England's no more a people!
    CROMWELL. Whose fault is that? Did I create the factions?
    VANE. Yours is the cleaving sword perpetuates them.
    CROMWELL. Say, rather, mine the cord that keeps them one.
    VANE. Such outward bond does but increase division.
    CROMWELL. What! when the dogs are mad, to drop the whip!

VANE. Since, while you hold it, madness does but grow.

CROMWELL. We talk like rhetoricians. Hear me, Harry.

VANE. Hear, you! 'Tis I must speak. At Preston Pans,
When God appeared in power, you sent me word,
Your heart new-flushed with pride of victory,
You did not like my principle of patience;
" This day be judge," you said, "'twixt you and me ! "
Then I was silent ; hear me answer now.
If to be patient mean to stand unshaken,
By that which action yields to interest,
Then be the judge 'twixt you and me the Lord !
'Twas liberty we both professed ; I've heard you
Loud in contempt of arbitrary practice,
In praise of Parliament and legal rule ;
Where's freedom now, where law ? 'Tis you whose action
Ruins the cause my patience still would raise.
The death of Charles I pass, if not approved,
At least not blamed ; from that time on, four years,
You served the Parliament, and then were great,
Though seeming to your baser self too small.
That council you expelled—dissolve you could not ;
Remained, for law, the soldiers, whose commands

Mere force made current; you, my lord, were chief,
And king in all but name. Were councils called,
'Twas but for swift dismissal did they touch
This new prerogative; men who'd spent their all
To serve the cause must fare as Royalists; all
But one small faction suffer, all submit.
Thus did the body politic of saints,
Christ their true head rejected, day by day,
Cleave into sects so multiplied that you
With outward force shall never more compact them
To inward vital union; no, the spirit
Died with the Parliament, and yours the sword,
Drawn once to smite its foes, that dealt the blow.
You had your will, and for reward control
By force of arms an anarchy of factions,
Whose only bond is common hate of you!
Your life will end your work, no son maintain
The throne you raised but could not 'stablish; Death,
With you involving yours, will leave a waste
Where England bloomed, and dim eclipse where blazed
The cause e'en men like you shall ne'er extinguish!
    CROMWELL. You talk of thrones—who wants to set
      them up?
Who calls me king? Who proffered me the title,
And who refused it? E'en if not refused,
Where were the treachery, the mean ambition?
Man, man, do you think to rule a State like this

By geometric axioms good for ever ?
Liberty's still your cry! what liberty,
Were I removed ?   The scaffold and the block
Under a second Charles !   You talk of factions,
Oh well you may !   But, on this heaved abysm
Of chaos self-tormented, who imposed
The law that, e'en from braying discord, strikes
To heaven's high court appealing harmonies ?
Vane, Vane, I lead no party, I lead the cause !
And if I lead, not follow, that's from God,
And under God ! 'twere madness to deny it.
Where could I stop ?   How without harm retire,
Or take the second place ?   From step to step
I was impelled ; to question meant destruction,
Not mine alone, but England's !   Think of it !
If I have erred—I have, what man has not ?
I know I must have, often, greatly ! yes,
But not as you think, not in purpose, never !
And let me tell you, Vane—you ought to know it—
There's more to mar our ends than human error ;
The grain of the world is curst ; there's flaws and knots;
Plane as you will you'll never plane it even ;
It's hard to blame the workman . . . .
Harry, my daughter's lately dead, and since
This burden's breaking me ; what use in words ?
Doubtless there's much to blame, and much to urge
In fair extenuation, but not now !

Now let us rather speak, like ancient comrades,
Of health and fortune, family and friends,
And all that still remains to sweeten life.
You're looking older, Harry; are you well?
    VANE. My lord, as you were friend to liberty,
So I to you; now that you use her name
Merely to cloak your own tyrannic ends,
I'm not so light a man to love the shell,
That houses now no more a kindred soul.
Your shifts and phrases touch me not; I leave you,
My message given, to conscience and to God.   [*Exit.*
    CROMWELL. Vane too, Vane too!
Yet, while I live, a thousand such as Vane
Shall never shake the power not I, but God,
Set up to quell his foes! And when I die,
(Which must be soon, so dissolution loads
My spark of life with ashes,) putting off
This weary, battered, too-perplexed being,
I'll dare expect, not owed but given of grace,
E'en to desert so small, the consummation
That stills at last this riddling sphinx of pain,
And rounds with heaven so jagged a world as ours.
But oh, my brother Vane, alas! my brother!

XIII.

Vane on the Scaffold.

June 2, 1662.

XIII.

(Voices in the crowd.)

"That's he, in black over the crimson waistcoat!
There in the cloak!" "That! why he looks as cheerful
As if he'd come to see the show himself!"
"Hark! what a noise! they're keeping back his servants!
Did you hear him? 'Not one servant to attend me!'
He seems surprised, not angry."

"What a figure!
And he a rebel!"

"Is he a rebel?"

"Hush,
They've made him one now." "Made him, you sour-faced rogue,
Why, he played third in Noll and Bradshaw's trio!
Who should be rebel, if he's not!"

"O, how I love
An execution! What a handsome gentleman!
He wears his curls like any cavalier."

"Heavens, what a crowd! Hush, hush—he's going to
   speak!"
VANE. [*Speaks from the scaffold.*] Gentlemen, fellow
   countrymen and Christians!
Why I am here you know, this huge assembly
Being met to see me, like a man in prison,
Take my discharge and pass to ampler light
Than peers through dungeon-crannies; on this
   stage
I make my last oration, asking only
Of you, my audience, a patient hearing.
First for myself; being bred, as others are,
A gentleman, I held companionship
With those good fellows whose discourse is dress,
Women, and arms, while with the wine ambition
They stuff their hearts to bursting; so did I,
Till something caught and tamed me, drew a bridle
Tight on my bitted mouth, and rode me forth
To wastes beyond the seas; wherein what hazards
I took from climate, want, and warring parties,
What perilous jars from man and monstrous nature,
Were long to tell; thence in good time discharged,
I found myself, not seeking, made a member
Of that great Parliament whose deeds shall live
While men have need of government. In that
   council

I, like the rest, being called upon to choose
'Twixt King and Commons, in such new disorder
Of powers co-ordinate like planets torn
Each from his sphere and clashed in red collision,
Held to the Parliament; whence came at first,
Though not desired, some place and influence,
Which how I used be all of you my judge!
If there be one can speak of private profit,
In wealth or station, trafficked in by me,
Or point to any man's estate or life
By me pursued as for my own advantage,
Now let him speak—let God speak if He knows!
None charges me! indeed 'twas rather loss
I met with later, when some men's ambition
(Whose heads wait mine to join them) seized the
    State;
Something I suffered in estate and person,
Yet for that cause which was and is—(I say it
Straight in the face of death and after-judgment)—
The cause of God and Christ!
    [*Interruptions in the crowd and on the scaffold.*
VANE. [*Proceeding.*]   Nay, hear me further!
Thrice was this cause declared; first, the Remonstrance
Painted in black and white the ship of State
On still upgath'ring waves of broken laws

Tossed to the rock Prerogative ; next, the Covenant,
Over two nations streaming, blazoned wide,
Flag-like, the church's sign—no pyramid
Goring with mitred peak, but crystal-sphered
Round the fire-centre Christ; last, fire and battle
Wrote it out large in act, whose issue cries
From heaps of dead to heaven ; such issue, friends,
As never any king—— [*Interruption.*
                    Right, Mr. Sheriff,
Enough of that ! now to the present business.
That I must die is little—nay, 'tis much,
The crown of all my labour ! For, in that chase
'Twixt man and death that folly nicknames life,
I have been still pursuer, death the fugitive,
Under whose goblin masque, a children's terror,
Plain I beheld an eyed and beaming splendour
Of sole immortal beauty. Death to shun
Were shunning life, possessed on that condition ;
For that all life is learning how to die
Is pagan lore, which we, with surer faith,
Were merely shamed could we not prove in action.
You will not think I boast ; 'twere late for that,
And hand and cheek would witness did I speak
Mere tott'ring words, unfounded on such rock
As roots within to base them ; I do not fear
Death, but to die a traitor—that I am not !

VANE ON THE SCAFFOLD.

(Nay, Mr. Sheriff, this does not touch the king.)
Much I could say and much, though hindered, have
    said,
How, when of three great branches whose one root
Is England's people, King and Lords and Commons,
Two were lopped off, one maimed, 'twas merest duty
To tend the rooted stump, wherein resided
The principle and origin of growth,
Past and to come; the superstructure crumbled,
Remained the fundament, whereon I base
My life and acts, the people! I say, the treachery
Was theirs who, being elected to that council,
Forsook their splendid trust; I say—'tis here
As at the trial—you will not hear me speak!
Nay, but you shall! You who refused me counsel,
Who stopped my mouth, who packed the jury, and
    swore
"Sir Henry Vane should be a sacrifice"—
'Twas Mr. Attorney said it—you who juggled
With the king's promised word to spare my life,
And played a farce with law to make me traitor,
You! Hear Sir Henry Vane to all mankind,
(Less for himself than those who suffer with him),
Against your courts to juster men unborn
Appealing, larger hearts and wiser judgments,
Protest their justice, innocence, and loyalty,

Who fought and died for England's cause and God's!
> [*Increasing interruptions; the Sheriff orders the trumpets to be blown in his face and snatches his notes away. When silence is restored* VANE *resumes.*]

That for the world; now for my friends alone!
The Cause you see is darkened—whether ourselves,
Some shrinking, some deceiving, be the occasion;
Or God, involving us in cheerless night,
Against that blackness more effulgent flashes
His face on worlds more blessed; yet from that night
Fire shall be born, e'en now perhaps is kindled,
And in my blood set free, from spirit to spirit
Unquenchable, till all be purged to Christ!
You know my hope, wherein I die content,
As men should die, happy, as Christians must.
I could have wished my life had been more quiet;
Faithful it was, and, to my measure, useful;
And, for my death, lend me your prayers to make it
Worthy of acts more notable than mine.

(*Voices in the crowd after the execution.*)
" He died well!"
" Like a prince!"
"The canting rebel,

He and red Noll will make a pair in hell."
" Did you see how still the head lay ? That's a sign
Of constancy in dying." " What is this Cause
He talks of ? "
"Cause ! Who knows ? Not he himself !
None of them know ! They're all alike these fanatics,
Live for a name and die for it ! "
" Lord, I thank Thee
For this Thy servant taken home to glory."
Mr. Pepys. [*From a balcony.*] " Lord, what a crowd !
Come, dinner, dinner, dinner ! "

> "I have spoken only to trees and stones, and had none to cry to, but with the prophet, 'Oh Earth, Earth, Earth!' to tell the very soil itself what her perverse inhabitants are deaf to."
>
> MILTON *in 1660*.

www.ingramcontent.com/pod-product-compliance
Lightning Source LLC
Chambersburg PA
CBHW020104170426
43199CB00009B/382